FIERY DARTS:

SATAN'S WEAPON OF CHOICE

THIRD EDITION

BY
JANET WARREN LANE

THIRD EDITION

ISBN: 9781936989225

Library of Congress Control Number: 2011935595

Published by

Certa PUBLISHING

P.O. Box 2839, Apopka, FL 32704

Printed in the United States of America

Above all, taking the shield of faith, with which you shall
be able to quench all the fiery darts of the wicked one.

— Ephesians 6:16, KJV

What readers are saying about
Fiery Darts: Satan's Weapon of Choice

"In a culture where fiery darts are constantly being thrown at us via TV, Internet, social media, and more, *Fiery Darts* gives us practical ways to combat them. Janet constantly points us back to the Word of God and points out how we must know God and His Word to fight the enemy. It is paramount to our walk with Christ to know the enemy's tactics and how to fight him. This book will be part of our homeschool curriculum next fall!"

Melissa Mathis, Homeschool Mom, Memphis, TN

"Janet Lane has captured key insights into spiritual warfare in her book *Fiery Darts*. She demonstrates how to overcome the strategy of Satan, who uses common reactions to the challenges of life to wound us and distract us from the calling God has given us to live in the beauty of His Kingdom through faith. Her book encourages us to live out the admonition of Romans 12:2: 'Do not be conformed to this world, but be transformed by the renewal of your mind, that by testing you discern what is the will of God, what is good and acceptable and perfect.' Lane emphasizes the intake of God's Word and the practice of prayer in this process of renewing our minds."

Linda Davie Moore, Pastor's wife, Hornersville, MO

"Fiery Darts is a biblical and practical primer on a subject area which impacts followers of Christ of all ages and cultures. The author's combination of scriptural insights and probing application questions earn this book a place in every disciple maker's library."

David Crane, Retired Southern Baptist Missionary

"The inner child in me cried as I read *Fiery Darts: Satan's Weapon of Choice*. My life would have been drastically different if I had this information when I was a young girl. All of my children have copies, and I am planning a Bible Study of the book with the young women in my church this fall. Thank you, Janet, for your obedience to Christ in getting this book in the hands of thousands. This little book is a BIG deal!"

Kellie Presgrove-Evins, Youth Leader,
Faith Baptist, Drummonds, TN

"The daily battle we endure is spiritual warfare. *Fiery Darts* provides practical action steps, so we can live the spirit-filled life. God did not intend for us to walk in darkness, defeat, or depression. This book is a firm reminder that we are free in Christ! Thank you, Janet, for encouraging us to put on the whole armor of God."

Cary E. Vaughn, CEO Love Worth Finding Ministries, Inc.

"Janet, a.k.a. 'Mama Lane' to those of us who know and love her well, brings such clarity to an area of our lives that needs clarity more than ever. In a generation that chooses to ignore the reality of a war that is eternal and cosmic in its implications, spiritual and literal in its repercussions, we need to be reminded that God has promised us discernment to fight well and defend well. The battle for holiness is a call that is worth fighting to pursue, and this book is a helpful weapon in that battle."

Brody Holloway, Snowbird Wilderness Outfitters

"There's a war and you're in it! Janet Lane's, *Fiery Darts* will shed light on the war around you, adding understanding and direction to stand firm. This powerful little book has shown me how to live effectively for God, wherever I go!"

Debra Moody, TN State Representative

Table of Contents

Acknowledgments

I would like to express a very warm thanks to my family for their support and encouragement in the writing of this book.

And for those of my church family of Faith Baptist and dear friends, who provided opportunities to share what God had been teaching me. You gave me the incentive I needed to follow God's lead towards publication.

To Certa Publishing, Jennifer and Monica especially.

To those who read *Fiery Darts* and found themselves equipped to identify the negative thoughts that were ruling their lives. Who then learned how to reject those thoughts and how to replace them with God's Truth thoughts. May you persevere in taking up your Shield of Faith in order to extinguish the fiery darts (negative thoughts) of the Evil one.

Finally, to Joney Caudill whose kindred Spirit encouraged me constantly and consistently to pursue sharing this life saving message.

Since the initial publication of *Fiery Darts: Satan's Weapon of Choice*, I have gained new insights in how to fight the fight against fiery darts more successfully. My blog, http://fierydarts.wordpress.com, chronicled much of this new information. Yet, there came a time when I realized that if these insights were included in my book, its message would be more clearly understood. Therefore, with the help of Certa Publishing in editing the original manuscript and adding points of clarification, *Fiery Darts: Satan's Weapon of Choice* has had a facelift (so to speak)!

My prayer is this newest edition will clear up any confusion you may have encountered as you were introduced to the subtle but powerful weapon of fiery darts.

Preface

The fact that God has a plan for our lives is common knowledge to most of us who call ourselves Christians. And with our birth into God's kingdom, discovering this plan becomes our primary focus. For those who become Christians early in life, this journey of discovery has the potential to be fraught with fewer detours than those who become Christians later on in life. Yet, no matter at what point our journey begins, Scripture is full of promises for our success. So, if success is our destiny, why are we, as God's army, plagued with such a lack of boldness and courage? Why are we so easily disheartened and distracted?

I don't really think there is just one answer to these questions, but I'm growing more convinced, day by day, that the following reason is significant in explaining our affliction. Could it be that we haven't taken into account that the Enemy has a plan as well? Scripture is clear in describing Satan's plan in John 10:10a (HCSB), *"A thief comes only to steal and to kill and to destroy."* So what is it that the Enemy desires to steal, kill, and destroy? The answer is obvious—anything God has planned for us!

The second half of John 10:10 reveals an aspect of God's plan for His children, *"I have come so that they may have life and have it in abundance."* The Enemy is not unfamiliar with God's plan. He knows his limitations, as described by Christ in John 10:29 (NIV), *"My Father, who has given them to me, is greater than all; no one can snatch them out of my Father's hand."* Therefore, the Enemy knows he must accurately choose his weapons.

I am quite certain that you know people who used to, from all appearances, be faithful followers of Christ (perhaps even church leaders), yet now, they no longer attend church. Their lives give little, if any, evidence of their former allegiance.

My heart breaks for those who have strayed away from the path they once walked on. What happened in their lives to lead them to deviate from a path that held nothing but hope and security for them?

And what about those who are in the church? Those whose devotion to God only motivates them to attend church, maybe even faithfully, but does little to impact their daily walk with Him? Yes, they have been born into the kingdom of God, but they have experienced little or sporadic growth. They know little of the power of God in their lives.

For too many years, my walk with God was characterized by more defeat than victory. Then, just a few years ago, I began to experience a gradual, yet powerful, transformation in my faith walk. As God continued to shed light on the darkness, which had plagued my walk with Him, I began to identify the source of my defeat. It became glaringly clear that negative thinking was at the core of my problematic walk with God.

It is the purpose of this book to expose such negative thinking, Satan's most useful weapon in demoralizing, weakening, and distracting God's army—you and me. And not only to expose the Enemy's weapon, but to make known the battle plan established by our Great Commander for defeating such a weapon.

In looking back on my journey, I have often pondered why it took so many years for me to reach the path that led me out of the darkness of my negative thinking. I may never know the answer to that question. But I do know that while my journey was lengthy, so were the lessons I learned. Also, I discovered that my struggles were not as unique to me, as I had so often thought. Indeed, as I began sharing with others concerning the quandary negative thinking had created for me, I found it to be a common struggle among many. Therefore, my hope is that by sharing the lessons I learned, your journey out of the darkness will not be nearly as lengthy as mine.

PART ONE

Chapter One

Introduction

Have you ever been a victim of your own thinking? Have thoughts ever paralyzed you or driven you to do something you knew was wrong or, at least, just not good for you? Are you susceptible to those who question the stand you take for God, to the point that you become more concerned with what they think than you do with what God thinks? Have you ever experienced the exhilaration of making a commitment to God, only to weaken in your resolve a short time later? Has confusion ever been so great in your mind that you found you were frozen in your steps, unable to move forward or even back to God? Do you find yourself growing less and less sensitive to sin? These types of questions are troubling to any believer, of course. And a walk of faith troubled by any or all of these questions can result in a life characterized by very few peaks and far too many valleys.

Satan has, at his disposal, a vast arsenal of weapons with which to wage war against God's people. While, it is obvious, he often draws upon weapons such as war, evil rulers, persecution, discrimination, poverty, adultery, murder, and broken homes, to highlight only a few, there is one weapon that is so subtle many Christians fail to recognize it as a weapon at all! This weapon is *negative thinking* or what I have come to call *fiery darts*—a weapon seemingly insignificant, yet incredibly dangerous. It is the purpose of this book to expose this weapon and reveal how its destructiveness can be subdued.

As God exposed Satan's weapons, or fiery darts, which he had skillfully used against me for years, my spiritual walk underwent a dramatic transformation. In teaching me what fiery darts were and how to counter their attack, my walk along the path God had called me to, so many years before, became illuminated. That illumination exposed Satan's tactics, and as I gained wisdom and strength in resisting the fiery darts of the Enemy, I found that my times of victory began to outnumber my times of defeat.

The first half of John 10:10 (HCSB) reveals Satan's intentions toward mankind, *"A thief comes only to steal and to kill and to destroy."* Once Satan's intentions were exposed and the tactics he had so skillfully used, which produced such defeat in my life, were revealed, my instruction on how to counter these attacks began in earnest. I was taught how to bring the power of God's Word to bear upon the fiery darts' assault. In so doing, the second half of John 10:10 (HCSB), *"I have come that they may have life and have it in abundance"* began to transform the character of my walk with God.

Chapter Two

The Strength of Knowing Your Enemy

Recently, the Lord led me to the sixth chapter of Nehemiah, where I discovered a vivid example of the power of being wise to an Enemy's motives. The book of Nehemiah is an account of the returning exiles from Babylonia—the third and last, and the one in which the wall was rebuilt. Nehemiah, the governor, had the responsibility of coordinating the rebuilding of the wall surrounding Jerusalem. The work was going well, in spite of much opposition through slander and treachery. Though the enemies were relentless, they did not take into account Nehemiah's strong reliance upon God, and each of their schemes was met with failure. Nehemiah set a dramatic example for all to follow in successfully fighting against the onslaught of fiery darts.

In examining Nehemiah's battle strategy, we come to understand the advantage that is ours when we become familiar with an enemy's motives. From Nehemiah 6:1-16, we can learn much regarding the strategy we need for combating our Enemy.

One of the first strategies of the Enemy, mentioned in chapter six of Nehemiah, was the plot to get Nehemiah away from his work.

Sanballat, Tobiah, Geshem, and the rest of our enemies heard that we had finished building the wall and that there were no gaps left in it, although we still had not set up the gates in the gateways. So Sanballat and Geshem sent me a message, suggesting that I meet with them in one of the villages in the Plain of Ono. This was a trick of theirs to try to harm me. (Nehemiah 6:1-2 GNB)

Under the guise of friendship, Sanballat and Geshem concealed their true motive, which was to harm Nehemiah. Had Nehemiah not been the man of prayer that he was, he wouldn't have seen through the guise of his supposed friends, and this trick would have been a greater temptation. However, Nehemiah recognized that the assignment he had been given by God had preeminence and should not be abandoned because of a friend's request.[2] Aware of the trick, Nehemiah answered accordingly, *"I sent messengers to say to them, 'I am doing important work and can't go down there. I am not going to let the work stop just to go and see you'"* (v. 3 GNB).

By leaving the task God had assigned him, even though the request was not noticeably dangerous, Nehemiah would have neglected the task and left the rebuilding vulnerable to an attack. However, Nehemiah's enemies were not to give up so easily and requested four more times that Nehemiah come to them.[3] Nehemiah 6:4 (GNB) said, *"They sent me the same message four times, and each time I sent them the same reply."*

What is the application for us in this account? We must be alert to Satan's subtle schemes to distract us from the task at hand. With a clear understanding of our assignment and a high level of commitment to that assignment, we will be more likely to recognize when Satan subtly tries to pull us away. Like Nehemiah, we'll know just what the Enemy is attempting to do.

How do we accomplish this? Clear communication with God, through prayer and His Word, will clarify the task and provide us with the confidence we need to perform it. When the Enemy comes against us with fiery darts, either in the form of thoughts or from those who don't value the commitment we have made to God, then through our newfound confidence, which we have gained through prayer and the application of Scripture, we will know what to do. Each time he tempts us, we can use the same reasoning Nehemiah used, "We will not leave our task just to come to you."

Verses 5-9 give the account of Sanballat's attempt to bring into question Nehemiah's intent. In an open letter, Sanballat wrote accusations regarding Nehemiah, stating that the Jews had plans to rebel and Nehemiah would make himself king. Of course, Sanballat, being the supposed friend that he was, sought to counsel with Nehemiah on how to address these accusations. If Nehemiah did not clear up this misunderstanding, then the Persian king would have to be alerted.[4]

Verses 8-9 (GNB) read, *"I sent a reply to him: 'Nothing of what you are saying is true. You have made it all up yourself.' They were trying to frighten us into stopping work. I prayed, 'But now, God, make me strong!'"* Nehemiah did not worry if his intentions had been misconstrued, but he depended upon God to protect his good name. He was wise to the Enemy's tactics and prayed for the strength he needed to continue the task and not be distracted.[5]

When we are not grounded in God's Word or aren't strong enough in our trust of God's provision and protection, giving in to such a temptation is all the more likely. We become vulnerable to the lies used against us, thus, increasing the possibility of succumbing to the temptation of giving up on what God has called us to do.

The Enemy's plan to stop the work had not changed. Nehemiah's assignment to rebuild the wall had not changed either. He had his mandate, and he would be faithful to follow through. He would not allow the libelous attacks of others to deter him from his work. When Satan uses others to hurt or harm us, we must stand firm. We must not allow the poison of their words or actions to seep into our thinking. It is in these times that we need to raise our shield of faith, which is the Word that God has given us, and move forward, armed with His TRUTH. The Enemy is relentless, as is revealed in verse 10 (GNB):

> *About this time I went to visit Shemaiah, the son of Delaiah and grandson of Mehetabel, who was unable to leave his house. He said to me, "You and I must go and hide together in the Holy Place of the Temple and lock the doors, because they are coming to kill you. Any night now they will come to kill you."*

Apparently Shemaiah was someone Nehemiah had some regard for, as is evidenced by the fact that he went to consult with him. However, when Shemaiah, the ambitious prophet, voiced his counsel, Nehemiah could clearly see the falsehood, and responded[6],

> *I answered, "I'm not the kind of person that runs and hides. Do you think I would try to save my life by hiding in the Temple? I won't do it." When I thought it over, I realized that God had not spoken to Shemaiah, but that Tobiah and Sanballat had bribed him to give me this warning. They hired him to frighten me into*

sinning, so that they could ruin my reputation and humiliate me. (Nehemiah 6:11-13 GNB)

Because Nehemiah was so close to God, he was able to recognize anything that did not appear to be of God. Therefore, the lesson we must grasp is that closeness to God is vital to our understanding of what the Enemy is up to and how we are to properly respond. Satan will not only use our own thinking to deceive us, but he will attempt to use others to foster that deception. Therefore, our closeness to God will be our greatest protection. By delving into Scripture for a word from God, the Enemy's plan will be exposed and we will have the ammunition to counter his attack.

In a miraculous feat, the wall was completed in fifty-two days and even Nehemiah's enemies had to admit that God had helped His people.[7] The completion of the wall had God's signature all over it, for this wasn't something that Nehemiah could have accomplished any other way. Sure Nehemiah was well guarded, but had he not bent his ear to God, man's protection would have failed him. It was God who alerted him to the tricks (fiery darts) of his enemies.

If applied, the lessons we learn from Nehemiah could provide some powerful alterations to our walk of faith. Nehemiah had a firm grasp of the assignment given to him by God and through constant communication with God, his course was clearly defined.

Unfortunately, our communication with God, through prayer and the study of His Word, may not measure up to Nehemiah's. I fear there are many who are still walking where I walked—in darkness. Too many Christians allow Satan's fiery darts to steal from them the potential strength and enlightenment that can come from the trials of life. In fact, our trials can add much to our walk of faith. Satan's design is to stop the work God has ordained for us, just as he attempted to do to Nehemiah.

By sharing with you what I have learned about fiery darts, I'm convinced your life can be transformed as mine has been. You will come to know more about the abundant life that God, through Jesus' visit on earth, gives us—a life every Christian should desire God's plan as stated in Jeremiah 29:11(NIV) is to prosper us, *"'For I know the plans I have for you', declares the LORD, 'plans to prosper you and not to harm you, plans to give you hope and a future,'"* and as previously quoted, to give us the abundant life mentioned in John 10:10.

I feel the problem could be that many of us know this, but we have failed to become familiar with the armor of God, which He has given us in order to stand against Satan's schemes. This armor is described in Ephesians 6:10-18 (ASV):

> *Finally, be strong in the Lord, and in the strength of his might. Put on the whole armor of God, that ye may be able to stand against the wiles of the devil. For our wrestling is not against flesh and blood, but against the principalities, against the powers, against the world-rulers of this darkness, against the spiritual hosts of wickedness in the heavenly places. Wherefore, take up the whole armor of God, that ye may be able to withstand in the evil day, and, having done all, to stand. Stand therefore, having girded your loins with truth, and having put on the breastplate of righteousness, and having shod your feet with the preparation of the gospel of peace;* **withal taking up the shield of faith, wherewith ye shall be able to quench all the fiery darts of the evil one.** *And take the*

helmet of salvation, and the sword of the Spirit,
which is the word of God: with all prayer and
supplication praying at all seasons in the Spirit,
and watching thereunto in all perseverance and
supplication for all the saints (emphasis added).

In this book we will focus on two of the pieces of that armor—the shield of faith and the sword of the Spirit. I am convinced that the Enemy's effort to keep us out of God's Word has been directly responsible for weakening the ranks within God's army, causing many to deviate from their walk of faith. There is no area of life immune to fiery darts. We are soldiers of the cross, but we have been trying to fight our battles without our shield and sword, and the results have been devastating. My prayer is that in revealing the fiery darts, thus exposing Satan's plan of destruction, individuals in God's army will pick up their shield and sword, sparking a revolution to reclaim the ground we have unwittingly given over to the Enemy (individually and as a whole).

Chapter Three

The Power of Negative Thinking

To say that negative thinking is powerful is an understatement! Yet, Satan has never underestimated such a power. Knowing full well the power of negative thinking, he has cleverly chosen this as one of his most effective weapons to carry out his plan to steal, kill, and destroy.

Psalm 13:2 and Psalm 55:1-2 pointedly describe the desperate position in which troubling thoughts can place us.

> *How long must I wrestle with my thoughts and every day have sorrow in my heart? How long will my enemy triumph over me?* (Psalm 13:2 NIV)

> *Listen to my prayer, O God, do not ignore my plea; hear me and answer me. My thoughts trouble me and I am distraught.* (Psalm 55:1-2 NIV)

What we think determines how we feel, and what we feel influences our actions. A negative action is often the result of negative thinking. Understandably, if Satan can negatively influence our thinking, then the temptation to act negatively will be hard for us to resist. Therefore, negative thinking, because of its destructive power, can be described as a weapon. A weapon Satan skillfully uses to dishearten individuals in God's army.

I find it intriguing that in the world of psychology we can find a parallel that supports the concept of fiery darts. It is referred to as "The Cognitive Triangle."

Negative thinking creates negative feelings, which create negative behavior:

THOUGHTS

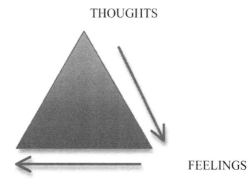

BEHAVIORS   FEELINGS

First we entertain a thought. That thought will cause certain related feelings. Thus, our behavior is influenced by our thoughts and feelings. Psychologists say that if behavior is to be changed, then the flow must be interrupted, either at the initial thought or at the feeling point.[1]

The parallel here is clear. When the negative thought occurs, it is at this precise point that we, as Christians, must analyze whether or not it is actually a fiery dart. If we determine that it is, then we need to bring God's Word to bear upon the thought, or fiery dart, to expose its lie. Once the lie has been exposed, we must reject it (by our will) and allow the TRUTH we have gleaned from God's Word to determine our behavior.

The comparison of negative thinking to fiery darts is striking. Both are small and subtle yet powerful in their destructive capacity. For most, the tendency would be to choose weapons that have the greatest destructive potential. A small dart by comparison would, therefore, be considered insignificant as a weapon.

My understanding of fiery darts did not come as a sudden explosion of light. It was more like a slow dawning. With this illumination, Satan's weapon, which he had successfully used against me, was exposed and the weapons God would have me use to counter attack were revealed. God's weapons had been available to me all along, but I had been in the dark as to how to use them. As Satan's plan and weapon became visible to me, I began to see, by God's training, how to use the weapons of His design to successfully counter the attack of fiery darts.

A realistic view of our areas of vulnerability, or weaknesses, in our flesh, or sin nature, is vital for understanding how the Enemy will attack us. While each of us may have different areas of vulnerability, we need to understand that our area of weakness will be the prime target for Satan's fiery darts.

Prior to learning about fiery darts, I had allowed influences other than God to muddle my thinking. Unfortunately, my times of defeat far outweighed my times of victories. But the good news is that we do not have to continue suffering defeat! Though we may have experienced much defeat, it is important to understand that we are God's children, and we have His seal upon our lives. The following verse reveals that Satan does not have the final word concerning us!

> *Do not gloat over me, my enemy! Though I have fallen, I will rise. Though I sit in darkness, the LORD will be my light.* (Micah 7:8 NIV)

During a Bible study a few years ago, it became apparent that I had a problem identifying Satan's lies.[2] The major reason for this was that I was not familiar enough with the Truth of God's Word. I discovered that five-minute, intermittent devotions, for years the characteristic of my time spent with God, was equivalent to not moving beyond the infant stage and drinking only milk. I had become spiritually malnourished and did not possess the strength I needed to distinguish good from evil.

> *Anyone who lives on milk, being still an infant, is not acquainted with the teaching about righteousness. But solid food is for the mature, who by constant use have trained themselves to distinguish good from evil.* (NIV Hebrews 5:13-14)

Because I was spiritually weak, I was easily confused as to what *truth* was, and a life of bondage was the outcome. John 8:32 (HCSB) says,

> *"You will know the truth, and the truth will set you free."*

I was not living in the freedom God desired for me, because I was not familiar enough with God's TRUTH—the most significant weapon in countering the attack of fiery darts. The outcome of that was a life lived in captivity. Therefore, I knew I needed to become more familiar with the weapon of God's Truth, so the light of that Truth would expose the lies of the fiery darts that Satan had been using to hold me captive.

That's what sparked my study of fiery darts. I made the connection between fiery darts and negative thoughts when my research revealed that evil thoughts and fiery darts are one in the same. Slowly the light began to dawn, and what had been hidden to me before was revealed. I finally began to recognize how I had allowed myself to be manipulated by Satan's fiery darts.

As I watched a video on the aforementioned study, I

wrote, "A negative thought that keeps me from obedience is not from God." I struggled with that statement. For if Satan was using my thoughts to hold me back from serving God, then why hadn't I been wise to that? After all, I had been a Christian for a number of years. You would think I would have recognized a lie from Satan. I began to understand that Satan knew I would reject an outright lie. Therefore, he had to do something to the lie, to make it palatable, so that I would swallow it. That's when it began to dawn on me how I had been manipulated.

Satan's tactic was exposed. It isn't new. He has been using it ever since the Garden of Eden. Remember how he manipulated Eve? Look at Genesis 3:2-5 (NIV):

> *The woman said to the serpent, "We may eat fruit from the trees in the garden, but God did say, You must not eat fruit from the tree that is in the middle of the garden, and you must not touch it, or you will die."*

> *"You will not surely die," the serpent said to the woman. "For God knows that when you eat of it your eyes will be opened, and you will be like God, knowing good and evil."*

Creating doubt in her mind, the Devil confused Eve, who was then unable to discern between the truth and the lie. We are still living with the ramifications of her choice. Satan continues to confuse us as to what is truth and what is a lie. I realized, by his taking a bit of truth and wrapping it around a lie, Satan had masterfully manipulated me into considering a corrupted version of the truth. My sensitivity toward the lie lessened with every temptation.

Another tactic to lessen my sensitivity toward the lie

was to tempt me to spend less and less time studying my Bible. Therefore, the further I distanced myself from the Truth of Scripture, the less likely it would be that I would recognize the lies from the fiery darts. As I relied less and less upon the Truth of Scripture to define my thinking, the lies influenced my thinking more and more.

Identifying the fiery darts, or negative thoughts, is vital to our effectiveness as Christians. Therefore, in the next chapter we will investigate this subtle but powerful weapon.

Chapter Three Journal Assignment

The purpose of this assignment is to assist you in identifying the fiery darts (i.e. negative thoughts) that you will be sure to experience this week.

I would like for you to take a few minutes and think about some of the negative thoughts you have had this past week, especially those thoughts that resulted in negative emotions such as confusion, doubt, anger, sadness, fear, indecisiveness, jealously, selfishness, irritation, or inferiority.

1. Record some of the negative emotions you have dealt with this past week or ones that plague you often.

2. Now, make a list of some of the negative thoughts that quickened those negative emotions.

3. In describing the negative emotion(s) produced by the negative thought(s) you mentioned, identify the attitude(s) and/or actions that resulted.

Chapter Four

Examination of a Fiery Dart

Now that the connection between negative thinking and
fiery darts has been established, let's take a closer look at the
weapon of fiery darts and examine their makeup. Merriam-
Webster's Dictionary defines darts as "a small missile, which
inflicts sudden pain." [1] In his commentary on Ephesians 6:16,
Matthew Henry compares Satan's temptations to darts and
uses "fiery" to describe the poisonous lies of those temptations:

> His temptations are called darts, because of
> their swift and undiscerned flight, and the deep
> wounds that they give to the soul; fiery darts,
> by way of allusion to the poisonous darts which
> were wont to inflame the parts which were
> wounded with them, and therefore were so
> called, as the serpents with poisonous stings are
> called fiery serpents. Violent temptations, by
> which the soul is set on fire of hell, are the darts
> which Satan shoots at us. [2]

Before Satan can be successful with the use of fiery darts,
he must do a little groundwork. As I mentioned in the latter
part of chapter two, in order for us to be desensitized toward
the lies of fiery darts, we must first have our understanding of
the Truth of Scripture diminished. By tempting us not to spend

time in God's Word, our ability to recognize the lies of fiery darts is equally diminished, if we give in to that temptation. In the place of God's Truth, the world's concept of truth (which is no truth at all) begins to define our thinking.

Now that we've identified the weapon, let's explore what it is about fiery darts that makes them so effective. The smallness of a dart makes it subtle, thus, dangerous. We tend to overlook its power because it is so small. When compared to a larger weapon, it doesn't appear to be much of a threat. For example, most would easily recognize adultery as an obvious weapon and would be able to resist the overt temptation. Therefore, Satan's plan of deception, to weaken one's resolve in resisting this obvious temptation, may begin with a seemingly innocent conversation. One conversation leading to others, coupled with the suspected victim's dwindling sensitivity to the dangers ahead (a result of not being in God's Word) is an affair just waiting to happen!

The poison, or lie, of a fiery dart of Satan's design is subtle. It is important that the lie hidden within the truth can be easily concealed. Continuing with the example, previously mentioned, one conversation may lead to others. A rendezvous may be arranged so the parties are able to converse more freely. Meeting somewhere for a conversation, or just taking advantage of some extra time to talk at work or at a meeting seems harmless enough. After all, friends can get together to talk with no ulterior motives. The subtlety is obvious—the danger is not!

Another important aspect to consider is that one or two of these low dose fiery darts would not be able to inflict much harm. In order for fiery darts of this nature to be effective, the Enemy must see to it that the darts continue to be fired off in a consistent pattern, producing the desired destructiveness. One conversation, leading to another, leading to a rendezvous, leading to a confession, leading to sympathy, leading to attempts to comfort, leading to a compromising arrangement, will inevitably lead to adultery.

Can you imagine the volley of fiery darts fired toward the parties involved in order for them to justify their actions? Also, the rate in which they are first encountered may be slow enough to not arouse any suspicion, but by the time things have gotten intense, the guilty parties are pulled in like a whirlpool, so fast they hardly know what hit them! Using this analogy, we understand how we can be caught unaware.

Perhaps we have taken the larger weapons of temptation more seriously: *"For from the heart come evil thoughts, murders, adulteries, sexual immoralities, thefts, false testimonies, blasphemies"* (Matthew 15:19 HCSB). What's going on in our heads? The thoughts we have, though not necessarily evil, aren't taken as seriously as these seemingly larger temptations. For example, the confusion that keeps us from taking a step of faith would not be thought of as a serious temptation when compared to something like the temptation of sexual immorality. So it's pretty clear why the subtlety of a fiery dart is such an effective weapon. Those initial thoughts, while not as alarming as something like sexual immorality, can lead to gross sin, if left unchecked.

As previously referred to, darts become deadly because of the poison placed on their tip. Consider this scenario: In the workplace, a man and a woman, who are not married to each other, decide to meet privately after several conversations. They have both confessed to experiencing marital problems. Making up this fiery dart is a lie cleverly hidden by a truth. **The lie is:** A man and woman, who are not married to each other, can meet privately and discuss their problems without any adverse effects. **The truth is:** It is helpful to discuss your problems with a friend. Yet this isn't God's Truth! Instead, it is a truth wrapped in a lie—a lie which proceeded from a mind controlled by the flesh, or sin nature. Perhaps we could classify it as "common sense" truth of the natural man.

Because of that common sense truth, we will entertain the thought, and the poison of the lie will permeate our thinking. It is the lie that will motivate our actions, which is contrary to God's will. These co-workers are focusing on the truth of going to a friend with a problem. Then the poisonous lie, that this is okay, will slowly seep into their subconscious in such a way, that their actions will soon become contrary to God's will. But because of the disguised truth, which hides the lie, they will not even realize that their own thoughts are being used against them.

Let me refresh your memory at this point: *For the fiery dart to be effective, Satan needs to remove the influence of the Truth of God's Word.* Remember Satan's scheme is to prevent his victims' thoughts to be cautioned, or influenced, by Scripture. For example, 1 Thessalonians 5:22 (KJV) says, *"Abstain from all appearance of evil."* If this Word was adhered to in our example, it would cause these individuals to avoid these compromising situations. As we become less and less familiar with the Truths of Scripture, our mindset, which is determined by a worldview and our experiences with the world, begin to make more and more sense. But remember, it is a corrupted truth, because it fails to recognize the standard of Truth, which is only found in God and in His Word! [3]

Whenever you are faced with a decision you feel God wants you to make, be assured that Satan is preparing the fiery darts to deter you. He will make sure that the fiery darts are so well disguised you will not suspect that you are struggling with a fiery dart.

Often, decisions of such a nature will require a step of faith. That means you can expect fiery darts designed to make you believe that you can accomplish the task God has set before you in your own strength. The fiery darts will be such that you will not be able to see your way clear to do whatever it is God has called you to do. You will begin to strategize and rationalize how you could accomplish God's will in your own strength. You may decide on a plan of your own design, with the intention of being able to, with that short-term plan, accomplish God's plan in the long run. The problem with this is that the short-term plan never accomplishes its desired goal. Instead of being just something you are going to do temporarily, it often takes on a more permanent nature. Thus, Satan has subtly stolen from you whatever God would have built into your life, had you been willing to take that step of faith.

You see, Satan does not want us to take a step of faith, just as he didn't want Abraham and Sarah to in Genesis 15. God had told Abraham that He would bless him with more descendants than Abraham could count. But his wife, Sarah, could not believe this was possible, because she hadn't borne Abraham any children. So what does she do? She came up with her own plan, which required little, if any, faith, to accomplish God's plan. Now, who do you think inspired that plan?

So why does Satan put up roadblocks when we attempt to take a step of faith? When you take that step of faith and move forward in obedience to what God has called you to do, even though you have no idea how He is going to provide and are maybe even a little fearful, you experience God's faithfulness in providing. Your faith then moves to a new level of strength. Your confidence in God being able to meet your needs increases, and you have a new aspect to your testimony concerning God's faithfulness. Not only is God glorified when you step out in faith, your act of obedience will encourage others as well. Now, it's pretty obvious why Satan would not want God's people to experience such things, because this would only strengthen and expand God's kingdom. That's the last thing Satan wants.

Never underestimate the power of fiery darts or their influence on our attitudes and actions. Their influence can render us weak and ineffective. By succumbing to the fiery darts, Satan has us just where he wants us. Being a part of God's army doesn't alarm Satan, if he can make us ineffectual by use of fiery darts. Can you imagine the damage that is done to the kingdom of God by ineffective, weakened Christians?

We must ask ourselves this question: *Have I allowed Satan to use me to cause damage to God's kingdom?* If Satan can deceive us into discounting the power of a fiery dart, and then add to that our unfamiliarity with God's Word (caused by a lack of realization of its power), is it any wonder why we fall prey to fiery darts and thus, become instruments of erosion in the kingdom?

Now that we have identified the weapon and have analyzed its makeup, the next chapter will show how Satan employs this weapon in the battle between the flesh and the world, in reference to the sources of our thoughts. The chapter will wrap up with how our new nature, given to us at salvation, equips us to overcome these battles.

Chapter Four Journal Assignment

The purpose of this assignment is to assist you in identifying the world's truths (little "t" not big "T") of your fiery darts and the lies that are concealed within the fiery darts, which you listed in your journal assignment in chapter three. Remember, *TRUTH* has little to do with the *truth* of a fiery dart! In the beginning, this may not be so obvious, but as you get more practice in identifying fiery darts, you will find the lies easier to identify.

MAKE UP OF A FIERY DART

1. *In the space provided, write the most troublesome fiery dart you listed in chapter three.*

2. *After examining this fiery dart, list the world's "truths" found in it.*

3. *Next make a list of the lies those "truths" conceal.*

Chapter Five

Be Aware of the Battles

We live in a world that no longer holds to absolute Truth. We can understand how those who hold a worldview apart from God would reject His Truth. But how is it that Christians are being deceived by Satan's lies? Remember, before Satan can be successful with the use of fiery darts, he must do a little groundwork. In order for us to be desensitized toward the lies of fiery darts, we must have our understanding of the Truths of Scripture diminished. When we don't spend enough time in God's Word, our ability to recognize the lies of fiery darts is equally diminished. In the place of God's Truth, the world's concept of truth generally begins to define our thinking.

In some cases, Satan's groundwork effort has been so complete, he has to do very little to disguise the lie. In those cases, Satan can present a temptation that is boldly and obviously contrary to God's Word and people will succumb to it without much hesitation.

How does this happen?

Of course, for those who have rejected God, it is obvious how they have been blinded to God's Truth. The world's concept of truth and their sinful nature defines truth for them and God's Truth bears little, if any, weight. Satan's job of manipulation, therefore, takes little effort.

But what about Christians? How have they been persuaded to defer to their flesh, or the world's concept of truth, instead of God's Truth? Again, it's simple but subtle.

When a person becomes a Christian they are given a new nature, one that is the direct opposite of their old nature. Formerly, their will was directed by their old nature, but at the point of salvation, their old nature was dethroned. Their will is now directed by their new nature. (This civil war is fully explained in Romans 8:1-11, see page 95.) With this comes a hunger to study the Bible and to maintain consistent communication with God through prayer. The old nature, the flesh, resists such desires. Eventually, Satan arrives on the scene with his first and most formidable fiery dart—tempting their old nature with powerful distractions, making it harder and harder for new believers to commit to consistent Bible study and time in prayer.

Satan is relentless in this temptation and as a result, an alarming number of believers succumb. Eventually, they find themselves on a road where they can receive no clear direction and their ability to recognize God's Truth is seriously compromised—right has become wrong and wrong has become right (Isaiah 5:20)! This is why Satan can throw a boldface lie at them without his deception being recognized. Scripture speaks directly to this,

> *For the time will come when they will not tolerate sound doctrine, but according to their own desires, will multiply teachers for themselves because they have an itch to hear something new. They will turn away from hearing the truth and will turn aside to myths.* (2 Timothy 4:3-4 HCSB)

> *They exchanged the truth of God for a lie,*

and worshiped and served something created instead of the Creator, who is praised forever. Amen. (Romans 1:25 HCSB)

Now the Spirit explicitly says that in later times some will depart from the faith, paying attention to deceitful spirits and the teachings of demons. (1 Timothy 4:1 HCSB)

For believers, the process of exchanging God's Truth for truth defined by our old nature, or the world's concept of truth, is deliberately slow and subtle. Of course, those who reject God altogether have no standard of absolute Truth upon which to gauge their life decisions. Their search for truths to live by is determined by what the world has to offer them.

As society leaves behind the Truth and drifts away from its former standard, we find that truth is subject to change. For example, fifty years ago, society, in general, felt the life of the unborn was to be protected whatever the cost! Not so today.

Today's self-absorbed society no longer considers the common good, benefiting society as a whole, when choosing standards. In the past, society's standards were based on biblical principles. But today, the private good of individuals, or particular groups, is the consideration when choosing standards, which aren't likely to be biblical.

Therefore, in order for certain individuals, for example, those embracing homosexuality and/or the pro-choice persuasion, to achieve the freedom to live out their chosen lifestyles (one that contradicts foundational principles), freedom, as it was known, was redefined. (For what they desire is more clearly defined as license.) By changing the definition (to the detriment of TRUTH), society was appeased. Because on a wide scale, having pulled away from God's Truth and no longer seeking His guidance in prayer, we have become blinded to this type of deception.

When our thoughts reflect less of what we are learning during our study of the Bible or what God's Spirit communicates to us in prayer then a downward progression is set in place, not just for individuals but for society, which is made up by those individuals, as well. Therefore, it behooves us to examine the sources from which our thoughts originate: the flesh, the world, the devil, and God.

The Flesh:

To put off your old self, which belongs to your former manner of life and is corrupt through deceitful desires, and to be renewed in the spirit of your minds, and to put on the new self, created after the likeness of God in true righteousness and holiness. (Ephesians 4:22-24 ESV)

Thanks be to God through Jesus Christ our Lord! So then, I myself serve the law of God with my mind, but with my flesh I serve the law of sin. (Romans 7:25 ESV)

The Battle of the Flesh

Before individuals accept Christ as their Savior, they are ruled by their flesh, or sinful nature—a nature predisposed to sin. However, when a person accepts Christ as his or her Savior, a new nature is born, ruled by God's Spirit. Yet the old spirit remains, thus, creating the great civil war that will be ongoing for the rest of their life.

Satan takes full advantage of the struggle between the old nature (the flesh) and the new nature (God's Spirit). His first attempt will be to weaken our new nature by tempting our old nature with distractions meant to diminish our desire to study the Bible or spend time with God in prayer.

If we allow ourselves to continue avoiding these two disciplines, then, our will is more easily influenced by our flesh and is drawn more to the world. Our attitudes and actions will begin to contradict the choice we made to follow Christ's example. The weaker we become in our Spirit, the more easily we can be manipulated by Satan's fiery darts.

The World:

Do not love the world or the things in the world. If anyone loves the world, the love of the Father is not in him. For all that is in the world—the desires of the flesh and the desires of the eyes and pride of life –is not from the Father but is from the world. (1 John 2:15-16 HCSB)

In their case the god of this world has blinded the minds of the unbelievers, to keep them from seeing the light of the gospel of the glory of Christ, who is the image of God. (2 Corinthians 4:4 ESV)

The Battle of the World

As for the "*world*," we mean the values and priorities, and the whole way of thinking of the unsaved population of this planet and the ungodly way in which they operate. That's because they all think, say, and do the opposite of what God wants a Christian to do. That's simply because the world is made up of billions of people who are all simultaneously operating in accordance with the values, standards, and priorities of their sinful flesh nature.

The world is rather like that because, when you

put all of that flesh together, you have an overall world system which operates in a remarkably consistent way. It constitutes and manifests the collective flesh nature of every sinner combined. Its consistency comes from the fact that they all have the same sinful, flesh nature. The problem is that, as we saw above, you and I still have that flesh nature too, even if we are real Christians.[1]

Christians, weakened in spirit, will not have the strength to stand against the world. It stands to reason, then, that the weaker Christians are spiritually, the more likely they will succumb to fiery dart attacks, designed to alter their attitude and actions toward what's going on in the world. Consider the rise in the acceptance of the homosexual lifestyle, for example.

The change toward acceptance of homosexuality began in the late 1980s after years of remaining relatively constant. In 1973, 70 percent of people felt same-sex relations are "always wrong," and in 1987, 75 percent held that view. By 2000, however, that number dropped to 54 percent and by 2010 was down to 43.5 percent. [2]

How do we explain this? Christians have clear instructions from the Bible that homosexuality is outside of God's will. So, if Satan can, by the use of thoughts (fiery darts), persuade a Christian who knows little of the whole council of God, to buy into the council of the world on the subject of homosexuality, we can understand the drop from 70 to 43.5 percent of those who feel same-sex relations are wrong.

The Devil:

In their case the god of this world has blinded the minds of the unbelievers, to keep them from seeing the light of the gospel of the glory of Christ, who is the image of God. (2 Corinthians 4:4 ESV)

For our battle is not against flesh and blood, but against the rulers, against the authorities, against the world powers of this darkness, against the spiritual forces of evil in the heavens. (Ephesians 6:12 HCSB)

Battle with the Devil

The problem, at least in the Western world, is that the majority of Christians either do not believe in the Devil or demons at all, or they do not believe that they are active in our lives or have any effect on us. Even amongst that minority of Christians who *do* believe that demons actively oppose us and influence us, there is still an element of unreality, such that demons don't *feel* real and are not taken as seriously as they should be.

This inability or unwillingness to take the demons seriously suits the Devil perfectly. He is very pleased when we deny or ignore their existence and activities. That failure or refusal to believe in them, or to take them seriously, enables them to get on with what they want to do, unseen and unresisted. Then the Christians whom they are attacking, tempting, undermining and deceiving are oblivious to what is going on. They attribute all adverse events and circumstances either to random chance or to other natural causes.[3]

In order for a Christian to fight this battle victoriously, Satan's existence must be acknowledged, along with his battle tactics and weapons. Once again, Christians not informed on what the Bible says about our Enemy, or how to counter his attacks, are doomed to his manipulation. He becomes the unrecognized Enemy that will defeat us, and we won't even know we've been attacked.

God:

For though we walk in the flesh, we are not waging war according to the flesh. For the weapons of our warfare are not of the flesh but have divine power to destroy strongholds. We destroy arguments and every lofty opinion raised against the knowledge of God, and take every thought captive to obey Christ, being ready to punish every disobedience, when your obedience is complete. (2 Corinthians 10:3-6 ESV)

I say then, walk by the Spirit and you will not carry out the desire of the flesh. For the flesh desires what is against the Spirit, and the Spirit desires what is against the flesh; these are opposed to each other, so that you don't do what you want. (Galatians 5:16-17 HCSB)

The God-Nature

In becoming Christians, we are equipped with everything we need to be victorious over the flesh, to recognize a worldview that rejects God, and to understand Satan's battle plan. As we delve into the Bible for the Truths contained therein, and as we spend time with God in prayer, we become more knowledgeable and more capable in resisting the Enemy. As we search for God's Truth and feed upon it, our new nature gains strength, and our spiritual maturity develops as our faith is established,

> *Therefore as you have received Christ Jesus the Lord, walk in Him, rooted and built up in Him and established in the faith, just as you were taught, overflowing with gratitude.* (Colossians 2:6-7 HCSB)

In addition, we learn about such things as the armor of God and in particular about the shield of faith, *"In every situation we take up the shield of faith and extinguish the fiery darts of the evil one"* (Ephesians 6:16 HCSB).

Now that we have identified the sources of our thoughts, in the next chapter we will spend some time learning how to tell the difference between a thought that comes from God versus a thought that comes from Satan.

Chapter Six

Telling the Difference

Now that the weapon of fiery darts and the scheme of the evil one (to steal, kill, and destroy) has been exposed, how do we, as Christians, protect ourselves? I believe it's important to understand that all the thoughts we entertain are not necessarily of our own making. Remember Satan's fiery darts? Our first line of defense then is to recognize the fiery darts. Recognizing a fiery dart was difficult for me at first, making it hard for me to make the right choice at times. However, the more I absorbed the Truth of God's Word, I discovered, my ability to recognize fiery darts steadily improved. My skill of using my Shield of Faith (to extinguish the fiery darts of the evil one) likewise increased. The Truth expressed in Ephesians 6:16 (HCSB) *"In every situation take the shield of faith and with it you will be able to extinguish the flaming arrows of the evil one,"* took on a new meaning for me.

So how do we recognize fiery darts? Examine the effect the "suspicious thought" has on you. Does it produce confusion, fear, doubt, anger, inferiority, indecisiveness, jealously, judgment, or selfishness, for example? It would be wise to consider where such thoughts could lead. For example, thoughts of self-sufficiency can lead to a decreased dependency on God. Thoughts of jealously could lead to revengeful actions. Thoughts of judgment toward ourselves or toward others fosters condemnation. (Remember, God convicts. He does not condemn.) *"Therefore, no condemnation now exists for those in Christ Jesus"* (Romans 8:1, HCSB) and *"For God did not send His Son into the world that He might condemn the world, but that the world might be saved through Him"*(John 3:17 HCSB). I'm sure you get the point.

These thoughts are designed for your destruction. Knowing that sin will certainly proceed from thoughts of this nature, Satan's plan to destroy us is set in motion. Therefore, if the thought's natural end is sin, it is obvious that Satan's fiery darts have been influencing your thinking.

It's vital that you keep in mind Satan's plan to steal, kill, and destroy. When a suspicious thought enters your mind, ask yourself this question, "If I consider this thought and act upon it, will good come from it?" If you cannot answer in the affirmative, then put up your shield of faith and stand your ground in deflecting such thinking!

On the other hand, consider Galatians 5:22-23. This is the familiar verse describing the fruits of the Spirit. When God puts a thought into your mind, then, love, joy, peace, patience, kindness, goodness, faithfulness, gentleness, or self-control, for example, is the desired end. The purpose behind thoughts influenced by God is meant to conform us into the image of His Son.

Likewise, we can know thoughts of this nature, when taken to their expected end, will produce life abundant in the things of Christ, which is the promise revealed in the second half of John 10:10. We can be confident that these thoughts can be traced to God and His influence, because making us more Christ-like is His plan. When you have determined the thought is a fiery dart, then put up your shield of faith (God's Word) and the fiery dart will be extinguished (Ephesians 6:16). Fighting off fiery darts with Scripture is effective!

Remember how Christ used Scripture when He was

tempted by Satan? Let's dissect these verses to highlight the truth vs. TRUTH component of the fiery darts encountered by Christ.

The Believer's Bible Commentary explains that the purpose of the temptations of Christ was to prove his worthiness to fulfill the purpose for which he had come into this world. In not yielding to Satan's fiery darts, Christ set the example for all of us in calling forth the power of God's Word to deflect such darts. [1]

Matthew 4:1-4 (KJV) deals with Satan tempting Jesus to turn stones into bread:

> *Then Jesus was led up by the Spirit into the wilderness to be tempted by the devil. And when He had fasted forty days and forty nights, afterward He was hungry. Now when the tempter came to Him, he said, "If You are the Son of God, command that these stones become bread." But He answered and said, "It is written, Man shall not live by bread alone, but by every word that proceeds from the mouth of God."*

Obviously, Jesus was extremely hungry after fasting for forty days and forty nights. Satan attempted to take advantage of this by suggesting Jesus turn stones into bread. Satan was clearly aware that Christ possessed the power to perform such an act. So, using the truth that in order for Christ to continue to live, He must eat, he hurled his first fiery dart. Once again, the Believer's Bible Commentary sums it up succinctly,

> Jesus answered the temptation by quoting the Word of God. Our Lord's example teaches that we don't have to live, but we do have to obey

God! Getting bread is not the most important thing in life. Obedience to every word of God is! Since Jesus had received no instructions from the Father to turn stones into bread, He would not act on His own and thus, obey Satan, no matter how intense His hunger.[2]

Therefore, the lie was that in order for Jesus to live, He must eat. You see, Satan would attempt to confuse us as to what we need in order to live. In examining this fiery dart, perhaps we should ask ourselves the question, "How do we define living?" Just staying alive is not necessarily living! Jesus knew that to *really* live, is to be obedient to every word from God. He tells us that He has come to give us life in abundance. Now that's really living!

Can you see how critical it is to know God's Word? Knowing the words that proceed from the mouth of God, in other words, the Bible, we have the TRUTH with which to combat the fiery darts from Satan. During times of weakness, our vision is not always clear, and we find ourselves vulnerable to fiery darts. It is in such times that we need to be able to call upon the strength available to us. Jesus set the example of what to do in times of weakness, when we are tempted. Only a firm grasp of the TRUTH of Scripture would enable someone being attacked by fiery darts (the sort Jesus had to deal with) to understand clearly the nature of the temptation.

Notice how Jesus responded to Satan's suggestion. Christ set the example for us to follow when a fiery dart is hurled our way. He quoted Scripture, in particular Genesis 8:3b (KJV): *"Man does not live on bread alone, but on every word that comes from the mouth of God."* Satan's fiery dart fell short of its intended target by the power of God's Word.

Now let's take a look at the temptation for Christ to throw himself off the top of the temple:

*Then the devil took Him up into the holy city, set
Him on the pinnacle of the temple, and said to
Him, "If You are the Son of God, throw Yourself
down. For it is written: He shall give His angels
charge over you, and in their hands they shall
bear you up, Lest you dash your foot against
a stone." Jesus said to him, "It is written
again, You shall not tempt the Lord your God."*
(Matthew 4:5-7 NKJV)

Satan got a little smarter here, using Scripture to add credence to his temptation. Unfortunately, it's not uncommon to hear a verse of Scripture being taken out of context to prove a point. It's called pretexting. This is exactly how Satan can use our unfamiliarity with Scripture to manipulate us into doing something that sounds holy but isn't.

According to Believer's Bible Commentary, Christ had the power to jump and escape unharmed, but to do so would have been to achieve personal glory by being disobedient to God's will.[3]

> Again, Christ resisted the attack by quoting
> Scripture: "It is written again, You shall not
> tempt the LORD your God" (see Deuteronomy
> 6:16). God had promised to preserve the
> Messiah, but that guarantee presupposed living
> in God's will. To claim the promise in an act of
> disobedience would be tempting God. The time
> would come when Jesus would be revealed as
> Messiah, but the cross must come first.[4]

Ever noticed how reluctant we are to suffer for Christ? Consider what James 1:2-4 has to say about suffering (whether it is of a physical nature or as specifically quoted in James):

Consider it a great joy, my brothers, whenever you experience various trials, knowing that the testing of your faith produces endurance. But endurance must do its complete work, so that you may be mature and complete lacking nothing.

Therefore, suffering is meant to equip our faith to endure the trials of life in order to mature us! By desiring that God remove our suffering, we shut ourselves off from the opportunity to learn how to become more like Christ and to be a testimony to others who are suffering.

(Sometimes God does remove our suffering, and I believe it's appropriate to ask that He do so. But in that asking, we must trust Him to do what is best for us (whether it be to remove the suffering or not) and be content to accept whatever answer we are given. Romans 8:28 anchors us in times like these.)

Plain and simple, we don't want to suffer. But honestly, do we really think that this life can be lived without suffering? Not really, so why do we recoil from it when it comes our way? The flesh is the culprit here!

So what's the "truth" vs. the "TRUTH" in this temptation? We can claim God's promises, certainly, but claiming God's promises presupposes that we are seeking His will. We are tempting God when we claim a promise in the midst of disobedience or impure motives. Thus, the reason Christ quoted the verse about tempting God. [5]

Consider the final temptation.

Again, the devil took Him up on an exceedingly high mountain, and showed Him all the kingdoms of the world and their glory. And he said to Him, "All these things I will give You if

You will fall down and worship me." Then Jesus said to him, "Away with you, Satan! For it is written, You shall worship the Lord your God, and Him only you shall serve." (Matthew 4:8-10 NKJV)

Satan would give Christ the world if He would only worship him! After all, 2 Corinthians 4:4 (NIV), *"The god of this age has blinded the minds of unbelievers, so that they cannot see the light of the gospel of the glory of Christ, who is the image of God,"* acknowledges that Satan is the god of this age. Yet, while he is powerful, we must never forget that he is not ALL powerful.[6]

Ever been tempted to compromise your walk with God in order to gain the world? Satan will tempt us to worship anything and everything in order to keep us from worshipping God. For example, how often do you find yourself tempted to watch television instead of having your quiet time with God? This is just a miniscule example, but think about how often you are distracted from doing something that will focus on God to focus on something of the world or yourself? Christ's response made it perfectly clear to Satan as to who deserved to be worshipped. From Christ's example we need to remember that only God is to be worshipped. So the "truth" that we must worship is obvious, but the "TRUTH" is that it must only be God. If Christ used Scripture to fight off the fiery darts of temptation, then all the more should we! When you are attacked, follow the example of Christ and find a Scripture that addresses the fiery dart and quote it back to Satan. You will find him fleeing just as he must do every time the TRUTH of God's Word is evoked. Therefore, like Christ, we should call upon God's Word when we need to discern "truth" from "TRUTH".

For example, since fiery darts are weapons that Satan

forms against us, a basic principle can be taken from Isaiah 54:17 (NIV), *"No weapon forged against you will prevail."* As I personalize this all-purpose verse and pray it back to God, the fiery dart fizzles in its power to defeat me.

In each occasion, we will discover our faith growing stronger. Our will is more clearly directed, and we discover increased skill in the use of our shield of faith. Chapter six reminds us that this is a lifelong process. A process that will result in the abundant life we all desire, as familiarity and obedience to God's Word increases.

Chapter Five Journal Assignment

The purpose of this assignment is to assist you in examining the fiery darts recorded in chapter four's assignment. The result will be the linking of Scriptures with the lie that is at the core of your fiery dart. *1. First, refer to the lists you made from the previous assignment (the list of "truths" and lies of your fiery dart). 2. Now, using a concordance, search the Scriptures for the TRUTHS that expose the fiery dart.*

Please note the following charts for assistance.

FIERY DARTS	GOD'S TRUTH	REFERENCES
It's impossible	All things are possible	Luke 18:27
I'm too tired.	I will give you rest	Matthew 11:28-30
Nobody really loves me.	I love you.	John 3:16
I can't go on.	My grace is sufficient	II Corinthians 12:9, Psalm 91:15
I can't figure things out.	I will direct your steps.	Proverbs 3:5-6
I can't do it.	You can do all things.	Philippians 4:13
I'm not able.	I am able.	2 Corinthians 9:8
It's not worth it.	It will be worth it.	Romans 8:28
I can't forgive myself.	I forgive you.	1 John 1:9, Romans 8:1
I can't manage.	I will supply all your needs.	Philippians 4:19
I'm afraid.	I have not given you a spirit of fear.	2 Timothy 1:7
I'm always worried and frustrated.	Cast all you cares on Me.	1 Peter 5:7
I'm not smart enough.	I will give you wisdom.	1 Corinthians 1:30
I feel all alone.	I will never leave you or forsake you.	Hebrews 13:5

Chapter Seven

Your Hope and Future

Finally, we must remember the importance of seeing things as they really are, not as we perceive them to be. We are instructed to take captive every thought and make it obedient to Christ in 2 Corinthians 10:4-5 (NIV),

> *The weapons we fight with are not the weapons of the world. On the contrary, they have divine power to demolish strongholds. We demolish arguments and every pretension that sets itself up against the knowledge of God, and we take captive every thought to make it obedient to Christ.*

Subjecting every thought to Christ, especially fiery darts, will expose the lies they encase. When we clearly see the weapon of the Enemy we can successfully fight against it. Second Samuel 22:36 (NIV) says, *"You give me your shield of victory; you stoop down to make me great."* As our faith increases, so will our skill in using the Shield of Faith. Also, remember that the mindset of truth promoted by the world will leave you defenseless and vulnerable to Satan's attacks, especially if you are not spending time studying the Bible. Not surprisingly, we will become victims of Satan's manipulation. We must examine our thoughts and ask God to reveal those thoughts that are influenced by Satan. The good news is that the more familiar we become with God's Word, the more determined our will becomes in choosing the way of Christ, as we ward off the Enemy's fiery darts with specific verses.

It is necessary that we understand that the Shield of Faith is made up of God's Word. Therefore, the power of God's Word, which we are able to access, is determined by the amount of God's Word that we have hidden in our heart.

It is also important that we understand that what we glean from Christian sources other than God's Word, must not be the major component of our Shield of Faith. What we have gleaned from God's Word for ourselves should be the major content of our Shield. Then, add to that what we have gleaned from other Christian sources, as we compare what they are teaching and how it measures up to God's Word. First John 4 says, *"Dear friends, do not believe every spirit, but test the spirits to see whether they are from God, because many false prophets have gone out into the world."* We must have a command of the Word of God, which will expose teachings that do not line up with the TRUTHS of God's Word.

Remember, our faith and will to choose God's way becomes stronger as we believe in and are obedient to God's Word. If we desire to successfully fight against the volley of fiery darts, which Satan will surely bring against us, then we must become more knowledgeable of the TRUTH found in God's Word. The TRUTH we gain from God's Word increases our sensitivity towards Satan's manipulation. We can more easily recognize the fiery darts as Satan's weapon, because we are gaining wisdom, through God's Word, for recognizing them.

And I feel the need to remind you that, sometimes, fiery darts are nothing more than subtle distractions. We think of them as nothing more than part of our natural thinking. For example, when we become overloaded with the demands of our "to-do" list or are unable to say no to other's wishes. In these moments, we lose our focus and cannot recognize our priorities. (Read the account of Martha and Mary from Luke 10:38 - 10:42, which illustrates this powerful Truth Thought.)

Please understand that this will be a lifelong process. Though that might sound disheartening, ask yourself this question, "Do I want to spend the rest of my life successfully warding off fiery darts, or do I want to remain a victim of them?" The answer is obvious.

Remember the TRUTH and its accompanying verse, which I shared with you in chapter three. Though I experienced much defeat, it is important to understand that I am a child of God's and I have His seal upon my life. When I am engaged in fighting off these fiery darts it's not Satan who determines the outcome of the battle. Remember Isaiah 54:17 (NIV), *"No weapon formed against us will prevail."* The Enemy has already been defeated, and though we may struggle in the battle, the final word from Micah 7:8 is that *"we will rise."* I would encourage you to remember that *you* choose victory or defeat. And know that by refusing to choose, you actually choose to fall and suffer defeat. Victory is yours as Deuteronomy 20:4 (NIV) reminds us, *"For the LORD your God is the one who goes with you to fight for you against your enemies to give you victory."* It is your choice! We know that Satan's plans are to destroy us, but take heart for God has plans for us as well. Jeremiah 29:11 (NIV), *"'For I know the plans I have for you,' declares the LORD, 'plans to prosper you and not to harm you, plans to give you hope and a future.'"*

I leave you with these words from Thomas à Kempis, 1380-1417, a Medieval Catholic monk and probable author of *The Imitation of Christ,* one of the best known Christian books on devotion:

Above all, we must be especially alert against the beginnings of temptation, for the enemy is more easily conquered if he is refused admittance to the mind and is met beyond the threshold when he knocks. Someone has said very aptly: 'Resist the beginnings; remedies come too late, when by long delay the evil has gained strength.' First, a mere thought comes to mind, then strong imagination, followed by pleasure, evil delight, and consent. Thus, because he is not resisted in the beginning, Satan gains full entry. And the longer a man delays in resisting, so much the weaker does he become each day, while the strength of the enemy grows against him.[1]

Chapter Seven Journal Assignment

The purpose of this final assignment is to encourage you to firmly establish your time alone with God. Prayer and God's Word is the most formidable weapon to successfully combat fiery darts—there is no substitute! Here are some suggestions:

- Get involved with Bible studies at your church whenever possible.
- Purchase a book of devotions and use it daily.
- Learn how to study the Bible.
- Be alert to the fiery darts that will surely come when you attempt to spend time in Bible study or take a step of faith. Be prepared!
- Obtain a concordance. A concordance has the added benefit of Hebrew and Greek dictionaries, an invaluable study tool.

I have also found a simple electronic concordance to be especially helpful when searching for verses to combat fiery darts. Or try doing an Internet search for a verse that relates to a struggle you may be having with a fiery dart/negative thought.

Using a commentary will add depth to your study. I suggest asking your pastor or trusted spiritual leader for recommendations.

Keep a journal of the fiery darts and the Scriptures used to combat them. This will give you much cause for praise and can be used as a reference for future struggles with fiery darts. It can also be used as a source to help others with their fiery dart struggles.

PART TWO

Applications

As I processed and applied the lessons God was teaching me for combating fiery darts, He turned my sight toward events in my past where I had succumbed to fiery darts. With each exposure, more light was cast and the end result was a revelation that was a bit overwhelming at first.

Satan's manipulation, unknown to me at the time, began in earnest when I was a young teenager. During that time of my life, I don't remember learning anything about Satan's use of fiery darts. Taking advantage of my lack of knowledge concerning fiery darts, Satan sowed the seeds of destruction, which would affect not only my relationship with God but every relationship I formed thereafter, and in particular, my future marriage.

What I desire to do in the second part of this book is to highlight two highly consequential times of life, in which Satan is able to target his fiery darts, relatively unhindered— the periods of adolescence and marriage. During these two periods of life, Satan has been free to carry out his evil scheme of manipulation and deception due, in large part, to the simple fact that we, as Christians, don't pray and study our Bible as we should!

That sounds like a major oversimplification, doesn't it? Yet, if you will continue to read, I hope to prove the soundness of such a statement. My intention is to expose the fiery darts with which we are attacked during the period of adolescence. Because it is during this critical time of our lives, on which the foundation of future relationships is built, that Satan has designed his most subtle fiery darts. Then, as we enter marriage with all the misconceptions stemming from the effects of the fiery darts sown during adolescence, Satan's plan to destroy our marriages takes root.

That's the bad news! The good news is that we possess the means to undo Satan's plan to sow the seeds of destruction during adolescence aimed to reap a harvest of failed marriages. By becoming a student of God's Word and communicating with God on a regular basis, we are in possession of everything we need to foil Satan's plan. It's that simple!

Chapter Eight

The Stirring of Adolescence

During the time of adolescence, there is a stirring that becomes keenly apparent to girls early on, and typically to the guys a bit later. It has been assumed by our society that this stirring heralds the beginning of "the search" for a future spouse, and as a result, girls and guys begin counting the days when they will become old enough to date. And, as our society relaxes its standards, the age to begin this search becomes younger and younger. When you add to that the ease of communication between our young people, guy/girl relationships develop in their intensity long before the individuals have reached a level of maturity to be able to handle such intensity.

The senses of young people are quickened to anything that speaks of romance. Our culture is quick to expose our adolescents to all sorts of romantic encounters on television, in movies, books, and depending on the ability of the adolescent to access it, it can be pretty graphic. During these encounters, our children are taught all about love and romance from society's perspective—a society that pretty much rejects anything God has to say on these matters. Then, they file this misinformation away into their memory banks and draw upon it as they become more and more consumed with the search.

Society's Approach

Let's examine the approach and result of understanding love as proposed by today's society. Our teens and young adults fall in and out of love with frequency in this search for their future spouse. And what do they learn from all this? Do they learn how to genuinely love and become prepared for their future marriage? Or have they unknowingly prepared themselves for a future divorce? After all, isn't that the pattern of dating? They meet someone, fall in love, and begin developing a relationship. When the relationship encounters a problem, it results in a break-up. Could it be that dating prepares them more for divorce than it does for marriage?

Dating is our culture's way, or practice, of searching for a future spouse in response to this stirring during adolescence. This bias is so ingrained into our thinking that we can't imagine encouraging our children to follow any other course. And as more and more adults become divorced, they, too, see no other alternative but to reenter the world of dating to find the fulfillment they believe can only be found in remarrying. Because this practice is the norm for our society, we are unaware that we have bought into something that has the potential to undermine and/or destroy any hope for future happiness or permanence in future relationships for ourselves and our children.

In Joshua Harris's book, *I Kissed Dating Goodbye*, he relates that at the turn of the twentieth century, a young girl and guy only became romantically involved if they planned on getting married. Then along came WWII and with the added influence of Hollywood, attitudes towards such things as dating began to shift. With this shift in attitude, came the arrival of the automobile, and suddenly, the old rules were outdated and new rules applied! Now young couples could indulge in all the thrills of romantic love, without any intention of marriage. They could enjoy all the romance they desired without having to be concerned with commitment.[1]

Consider how the practice of dating affects our concept of romantic love. Isn't it pretty much self-centered? It's an "all about me" mentality, so that by the time our children reach marrying age, they are so bruised and battered by break ups, they are ill-equipped to identify or exhibit the characteristics of true love. And when they decide to get married, based on their previous experiences, what kind of security do they have that their marriage will last?

I think most of us realize that there are some serious flaws with the practice of dating as dictated by our society, we, therefore, attempt to modify it to counteract those flaws. So Christian parents attempt to make adjustments to protect their children, which is a good and necessary thing.

The Adamic Curse

It is obvious that relationship-building is a struggle for most, and there is a scriptural explanation as to why. Genesis 3:16 (NIV) gives insight into this,

> *To the woman he said, "I will greatly increase your pains in childbearing; with pain you will give birth to children. Your desire will be for your husband, and he will rule over you."*

Because of the Adamic curse, everything in this world serves our flesh. Therefore, relationships will exist to serve our wants and needs. Men and women, without the intervention of Christ, see marriage from a perspective centered on self. The word "desire" in verse 16 is defined as reaching after something desperately. If we have not had that desperate longing fulfilled in a relationship with Christ, as women in particular, we will seek desperately to find that fulfillment in a romantic relationship. [2]

The Stirring – According to God

Remember in Part One, I said that Satan has a plan for our lives and that is to kill, steal, and destroy whatever it is that God has planned for us. Let's go back to that "stirring" I mentioned earlier. Could it be that the stirring in our heart, which initiates a search for true love, is the Holy Spirit calling us to a love relationship with our Creator? I think so! Why else would Satan enforce a plan to do everything he could to make sure that we misunderstand what this stirring encompasses?

If in those early years, we set our focus on cooperating with God as He teaches us the true meaning of love, then our future attitudes and actions will reflect an appropriate definition of love, because our textbook is God's Word. In particular, verses like 1 Corinthians 13:1-7. (See page 94.) We could do nothing better to prepare ourselves to live life and love others (especially our future spouse) successfully, than studying and applying the Truth about love from the book written by the author of love!

If we could be grounded in our understanding of true love, by spending time learning about true love from the very source of true love, God, then we would enter relationships as whole, healthy, and complete individuals. We would handle problems we encounter in those relationships from a healthy perspective. Having been taught to recognize genuine love, we would avoid relationships that offered anything less.

Reconsider the effect of the Adamic curse. Society tells us that we need to search, which means dating, for someone who will complete us, someone that will make us happy. If we buy into this thought, then Satan has no trouble fashioning a most deceptive fiery dart that will convince us that, as individuals, we are incomplete and we need the love of another person to make us whole. This fiery dart assumes that we do not realize it is the love of God which completes us and makes us whole, not a romantic relationship with someone of the opposite sex.

But God's plan is that He is to be the fulfillment of that desire; the desire a woman has under the curse. That is something, as women, we need to learn early on, the earlier the better, preferably during adolescence, but especially before we get married. No one else is capable of fulfilling that desire—no boyfriend, no father, and no husband. This desire can only be fulfilled in Christ.

Therefore, when our relationship in Christ is firmly established, then we will not be expecting a father, a boyfriend, or a husband to do for us what only Christ can do. We will release them from the prison of unrealistic expectations in which we have held them.

Results of Cooperating with God's Plan

Adolescence is the perfect time in our lives to become acquainted with a life lived passionately for Christ. When our first love is Jesus Christ, and we discover that He totally fulfills our desires, then we develop a healthy definition of true love. The foundation of understanding love is firmly established. So that by the time we meet Mr. or Miss Right, we approach the relationship having experienced the true love of Christ, and we will be less likely to carry unrealistic expectations into our new relationship.

When we have a clear understanding of true love, then much can change in our lives. Depending on our level of understanding, we may *need* to make some changes. We may change things like what we wear, our attitudes, our activities, our speech, the manner in which we behave toward others, or even our choice of friends. When we are motivated by a pure love for God, then we will want to please Him in all our ways. First Thessalonians 4:1a (NIV) points out, *"Finally, brothers, we instructed you how to live in order to please God."* When we, therefore, identify things in our lives that don't please God, we will desire to eliminate those things. And when God impresses upon us something that needs to be eliminated, we can trust Him to help us recognize the fiery darts that persuaded us to give in to such things.

God's plan is to teach us how to love, so that we will be whole and complete in Him. In that state, we will be passionate about Him, and pleasing Him will be our priority. Our desire will be to cooperate with God as He conforms us into the image of Christ. We will desire to do those things that please Him, and we will trust Him to lead us down the path He has planned for our lives, knowing that He is totally capable of making us happy. We will be able to resist the fiery darts that are attempting to get us off track. We will be willing to stand alone, if need be, for we are keenly aware of what the Enemy is up to. The desire to be accepted and/or popular, which is ruled by the flesh, is seen for the fiery dart it is. We will know that making choices to follow after the things of this world, will only lead to bondage. Making the choice to follow after God's Truth, will lead to freedom. John 8:32 (HCSB), *"You will know the truth, and the truth will set you free."*

Since our focus will be to please God, we will trust Him to conduct "the search" for us. We will then be spared the overwhelming stress and pain that taking on such a burdensome task can bring. Therefore, when the time comes for Him to introduce us to our future spouse, we will only be attracted to someone who is a complete and whole individual in Christ. Likewise, since we are complete and whole individuals in Christ ourselves, we won't need for another individual to do for us what God has already done.

Results of Cooperating with Satan's Plan

Yet, when we succumb to Satan's fiery darts, it creates confusion and misunderstanding that will direct us to the opposite path God intended—a path that will take us further and further from the Truth of God. This is the exact opposite of what we learn about true love, as we sit at Jesus' feet. The fiery darts will be the culprit that will keep us from distinguishing truth (with a small "t") from Truth (with a capital "T").

Society's way of defining love should not be the source for our definition. In Isaiah 55:8-9 (NIV), God cautions us with these words,

> *For my thoughts are not your thoughts, neither are your ways my ways, declares the LORD. As the heavens are higher than the earth, so are my ways higher than your ways and my thoughts than your thoughts.*

By allowing society's thoughts, or worldview, to hold a greater influence over our thinking and behavior regarding love, Satan will use this to fashion fiery darts meant to keep us from desiring and achieving the higher purpose God intended. God's Word concerning love, when understood and applied, will reap the abundant life He desires and has planned for us.

Alternative Plan

The way dating is approached in our country, should not be the way those within the church should approach it. If we are bold enough to examine this practice, we will uncover, hidden within its framework, more fiery darts than we could imagine. That should be all we need to reject the world's approach to dating and to seek God's plan concerning dating. Believe it or not, there are fabulous alternatives to the practice of dating. But we have been blinded by fiery darts and just couldn't see them.

As you allow God's Word to reinstruct you in how to approach forming relationships during the teen years, you will discover there is no parallel for dating in the Bible. Now don't close this book! For it will be to your benefit to become aware of God's alternative found in courtship. And with the renewed interest in courtship, you won't have any trouble finding plenty of sources to renew your thinking and to prepare yourself for a marriage more likely to know the permanence and fulfillment God has designed for such a union.

Now, what if you find yourself some distance away from the path of God's design and, as a result, have suffered one broken relationship after another? Stop, right where you are and pray for the knowledge you need to change your course. The wonder of God's love is that He is willing to take you right where you are and lead you back to the path He designed for you. Of course, Satan will try to convince you otherwise, but remember those thoughts are fiery darts and Satan is an eternal liar!

Conclusion

If Satan can keep us confused with fiery darts about how to live life as an adolescent, then from that unstable foundation, we will live life and make choices that will set us on a path of destruction, in particular in marriage.

Therefore, in the next application we will take a look at the fiery darts Satan has designed to stir up the seeds of confusion in marriage, which were sown during our adolescence. But, just as we have received the good news of how to redeem the period of adolescence, we will also learn the good news of how to redeem the marriage relationship.

Chapter Nine

The Fiery Darts in Marriage

Satan has some cunningly devised fiery darts for those who come out of their period of adolescence not having the definition of love (as revealed by God) clearly defined. They enter into a marriage fueled, for the most part, by a romantic, idealistic perception of love. These fiery darts are designed to ensure that we remain in the dark when it comes to understanding and experiencing God's plan for marriage.

The Basis for our Vulnerability

Before going any further, let me reiterate. There are two factors to Satan's successful use of fiery darts to which you must always be alert. If he can keep you from consistent Bible study and prayer, then you will not possess the ability to recognize the lies of fiery darts, and your thinking will be vulnerable to Satan's manipulation.

Recently, God has added to my understanding another aspect of why Satan desires to keep us out of God's Word and to keep us from prayer. I discovered this as I studied the book *The Holiest of All*, a commentary on the book of Hebrew by Andrew Murray, a South African Dutch Reformed Missionary of the late 1800s. In the preface of this book, I came across this passage: "Those who, through sloth, remain babes in Christ, and do not press on to maturity, are ever in danger of hardening their heart, of coming short and falling away."[1]

As Christians, our goal should be to grow in our knowledge of Christ, so that we can become more like Him. When we are experiencing consistent nourishment from God's Word and prayer, then our spiritual health will increase. As a result, this next passage from the *The Holiest of All* will come to describe our lives:

> The knowledge of the heavenly character of Christ's person and work is what alone can make heavenly Christians, who, amid all the difficulties and temptations of life on earth, can live as those whom the superior power of the upper world has possessed, and in whom it can always give the victory."[2]

By keeping us from God's Word and time in prayer, Satan ensures that we will not mature in our relationship with Christ, which explains why we live in such defeat. It also explains why we are so easily deceived during adolescence and why our marriages do not live up to God's expectations. I cannot emphasize this strongly enough: **Leaving these two factors—the study of God's Word and time in prayer—out of your marriage relationship, is setting the stage for disaster.**

The more we pray and the more we study, the more of Christ is revealed to us. Our faith is strengthened and our access to the power of God is increased. Our ability to recognize fiery darts becomes keener, and we do not succumb to their influences so readily. We will recognize the battle going on between our flesh and our spirit and we will choose to cooperate with God's plan instead.

The fact that you are reading this book shows that you desire to know more about Christ. You recognize that the problems you encounter in your life will have their solutions in Him. But books such as this, without a follow up of personal Bible study and prayer, will produce limited success, at best. Though books designed to inspire your spiritual growth are important, they are not to be the whole of your effort, but instead, they are designed to give you a point of reference from where God wants to prepare you to learn more about Christ.

When these two disciplines, Bible study and prayer, are not practiced consistently in a Christian's life, Satan's fiery darts find an easy mark, especially within the realm of marriage. With the powerful influences exerted upon us from a society, which is completely devoid of understanding of God's plan for marriage, we put our marriages severely at risk when we don't practice the discipline of studying God's Word and spending time in prayer.

Everyone who is, or has been, married will attest to the fact that maintaining a healthy relationship seems all but impossible at times. There are too many distractions in the climate we live in today that serve to pull couples apart. These distractions and fiery darts serve to prevent couples from dealing with their problems in a healthy manner and the results have been disastrous. Sadly, 40 to 50 percent of the marriages in America today end in divorce. Unfortunately, the statistics aren't much better for Christian marriages.[3]

This is a sad commentary on our times. Where have we gone wrong and is there anything we can do to change things for the better? I, wholeheartedly, believe that there is much we can do to change things for the better. As a matter of fact, it is God's plan! One of the most important things we need to do is to redefine our thinking in two areas. In the last chapter, I talked about one of those areas, the period of adolescence and what we were to learn there. The second area where we need to redefine our thinking is in the area of marriage.

Misconceptions

Marriages today are in trouble. Most enter into marriage with the hope that it will be forever, but are ill-equipped with the tools that will ensure such permanence. The romantic, idealistic perception of love that laid the foundation of too many marriages is hardly strong enough to bear up under the onslaught of today's temptations.

No one would deny the highly successful attacks Satan orchestrates when it comes to marriage. Remember, in the study of fiery darts, when Satan can keep you from a consistent dependence upon prayer and God's Word, then you will be a prime target for fiery darts. Christians like this have a tendency to allow the wisdom of the world to have too much to do with how they define marriage. Let's consider some definitions of marriage from a website entitled, *Save Your Marriage Center:*

- *The purpose of marriage is to bind one another together in love. To help each other perfect themselves and stay on the path that will lead them to the most happiness.*

- *It encompasses and is built upon sexual, physical, economic, emotional, charitable, and spiritual bond.*

- *Married people agree to limit their behavior in all areas in concert with the agreed-on limits of the marriage.*

- *Marriage is not about sex, love, or happiness. Marriage is the basic building block of society in that it creates stability for its members and that of the future generations, and therefore society as a whole. Maintaining love in marriage by the avoidance of harm and the meeting of needs is the mortar that holds the commitment to the union together.*

- *Loss of love is not reason for dissolution of the marriage but a call to explore how to restore that love and one's own need for change within the marriage.*[4]

(The last one sounds good, talks about commitment, which is very good, but it is flawed because it is man-centered.)

On a certain level, all of these definitions contain wisdom, and that is exactly why I refer to them as fiery darts. As a matter of fact, if we were to be honest with ourselves, there are a few of them that we have bought into wholeheartedly. Do you know how this happened?

When we have a constant diet of television, movies, romantic novels, and/or music that contain, at their core, these definitions of marriage, and that outweighs the influence of God's Word in defining marriage, the resulting effect is a foundation laid without substance. The divorce rate in the church almost equals the divorce rate outside the church, which provides evidence that Satan's plan to steal, kill, and destroy, is achieving disastrous results.

Why are marriages within the Church breaking up at a rate almost equal to those outside of the church? Could it be that fiery darts have so invaded our thinking that we have lost sight of the purpose of marriage as designed by God?

Let me refresh your memory about something from chapter six. Genesis 3:16 (NIV) reads,

> *To the woman he said, "I will greatly increase your pains in childbearing; with pain you will give birth to children. Your desire will be for your husband, and he will rule over you."*

Because of the Adamic curse everything in this world serves our flesh. Therefore, relationships will exist to serve our wants and needs. This is why the fiery dart that "marriage exists to make us happy" is so powerful.

Yet, when we become a child of God and our growth process begins, we will come to understand that this attitude is the consequence of sin. We will also learn, if we avail ourselves to the teaching of it, that marriage is designed for something far more beautiful and loftier than society is equipped to understand.

Purpose of Marriage

It is a familiar theology that Christ should be at the center of our marriage. We possess a certain level of understanding that marriage is a picture of the relationship between Christ and His church. But while we are familiar with it, can we truly say we understand what that looks like in a marriage? We all know that Christ is to be the center of the marriage, but do we truly understand what that looks like? Because of fiery darts, I think, it is likely, that lurking within our understanding is a major dose of misunderstanding!

Something basic to living life as a Christian must be nailed down here before we can successfully move forward. The purpose for which we exist is to be conformed into the image of Christ. Consider Colossians 3:9-10 (GNB):

> *Do not lie to one another, for you have taken off the old self with its habits and have put on the new self. This is the new being which God, its Creator, is constantly renewing in his own image, in order to bring you to a full knowledge of himself.*

This means that everything and every relationship in our experience exist to serve the purpose of conforming us into God's image, in order to bring us into a full knowledge of Himself. As we become more like Christ, we are going to grow into a fuller knowledge of God.

So, how does the purpose for which we are to exist relate to the purpose of marriage? In the book entitled *Sacred Marriage,* by Gary Thomas, an intriguing question is asked, "What if God designed marriage to make us holy more than to make us happy?"[5]

Therefore, if marriage is designed to make us holy, then that involves us conforming to the image of Christ. But how is that accomplished? Scripture answers this by pointing out that marriage is a picture of the relationship between Christ and His Church. Ephesians 5:25-26 (NIV):

> *Husbands, love your wives, just as Christ loved the church and gave himself up for her to make her holy, cleansing her by the washing with water through the word, and to present her to himself as a radiant church, without stain or wrinkle or any other blemish, but holy and blameless.*

Christ loves the Church and sanctifies her, therefore, as Christians we are to submit to that sanctification process. Consider Ephesians 5:22-32 (NIV),

> *Wives, submit to your husbands as to the Lord. For the husband is the head of the wife as Christ is the head of the church, his body, of which he is the Savior. Now as the church submits to Christ, so also wives should submit to their husbands in everything. In this same way, husbands ought to love their wives as their own bodies. He who loves his wife loves himself. After all, no one ever hated his own body, but he feeds and cares for it, just as Christ does the church - for we are*

members of his body. For this reason a man will leave his father and mother and be united to his wife, and the two will become one flesh. This is a profound mystery - but I am talking about Christ and the church. However, each one of you also must love his wife as he loves himself, and the wife must respect her husband.

The husband, then, is to love his wife using the way in which Christ loved the church as his blueprint and the wife is to respect her husband using the church's submission to Christ as her blueprint. The sanctification process, that is the process of making us holy, is the motivation for the husband to love his wife and the wife to respect her husband. When you see yourself and your spouse as objects of sanctification, then how you treat each other will be defined by that understanding.

In my research, I came across this statement from an excerpt entitled, *Help for the Struggling Marriage* by Reb Bradley,

> To evaluate our personal success in a marriage we must not then look to see if our needs are being met, but we must ask ourselves, "Am I demonstrating the image and character of Jesus Christ?' God knows that as we grow into the image of Jesus our greatest needs are met."[6]

It is the problems we encounter in our marriage and the manner in which we respond to them that can make us holy, conforming us into the image of Christ. In his book, Gary Thomas asks this question, "Would I rather live a life of ease and comfort and remain immature in Christ, or am I willing to be seasoned with suffering if by doing so I am conformed to the image of Christ?"[7]

Unfortunately, we live in a land that abhors suffering. We desire a life of ease, one free from suffering. The fiery dart of such thinking sees suffering as something to be avoided, certainly not something to be embraced. However, the reality is that we live in a world that suffers. Every marriage, to some degree, experiences suffering. So, doesn't it make sense that we should come to terms with the part suffering plays in conforming us into the image of Christ?

Our attitude toward suffering will undergo a change when we face life, or in this case, marriage, with the understanding that at some point we are going to encounter some type of suffering. If we respond rightly to this suffering, we will become more like Christ, and this will strengthen our marriage. Instead of being overwhelmed by our suffering, we will find that we can deal with the unhappiness that accompanies such suffering. We will use our unhappiness to reveal our sin and hurtful attitudes, which will result in exposing the fiery darts to which we have fallen prey. In the process, we will discover that we have a peace that surpasses all understanding, and we will know the happiness we've longed for, even if our marriage isn't going so well.

If our marriage is built upon the foundation of God's design, we will understand that there will be times when we will be unhappy in our marriage and/or with our spouse. This is a reality that will be dealt with in a godly manner so that it does not become an excuse to bail out but an instrument of God's will in conforming us into His image. This is what centering your marriage on Christ means. As Brody Holloway, my good friend and a leader of a Christian youth camp in North Carolina, put it at a marriage retreat there, "Frustration, hardship, loss is rooted in the gospel. In that context (centering your marriage on Christ) your faith may be shaken but your marriage will remain rooted." [8]

You see, the type of suffering, or problems, we

encounter in our marriages will often reflect something that is lacking therein. It stands to reason, then, that if we cooperate with the sanctification process in order to provide what is lacking in the marriage, we aren't likely to see breaking up the marriage as the solution. James 1:2-4 (NIV) makes this quite clear:

> *Consider it pure joy, my brothers, whenever you face trials of many kinds, because you know that the testing of your faith develops perseverance. Perseverance must finish its work so that you may be mature and complete, not lacking anything.*

The Difference Understanding God's Design Makes

When a marriage lacks "love," as defined by society (i.e. romantic feelings), it becomes inconceivable to those subscribing to society's definition of love to remain in the relationship. When it is romance that fuels our relationship, then our focus is on the performance, or lack thereof, of our spouse. Because we are consumed with highlighting our spouse's faults, instead of coming to terms with what there is to learn from the book of James, we miss out on an opportunity to discover the truth about love, which, obviously, our marriage lacked. A truth that we would have been first exposed to during adolescence, had we studied what Scripture teaches us about defining love, according to that source's definition.

In defining love, could it be that we have succumbed to another fiery dart? When we define love according to 1 Corinthians 13:4-7 (NIV), we find that,

> *Love is patient and kind; it is not jealous or conceited or proud; love is not ill-mannered or*

selfish or irritable; love does not keep a record of wrongs; love is not happy with evil, but is happy with the truth. Love never gives up; and its faith, hope, and patience never fail.

This is the kind of love Jesus has for us. It is a God-centered view of love. This kind of love will preserve a marriage, because it brings glory to God and points a sinful world to the reconciling love of its Creator.[9] Do we think that we could love like this if we had never encountered the situations with the potential to teach us how to love in this manner? This love is not performance based. It does not require that our earthly comforts, desires, and expectations, be met. It is not self-seeking, which unfortunately, defines, for too many of us, the basis of our love for others. This type of love can only be found by sitting at the feet of Jesus and allowing Him to teach us how to love as He loves.

A clear understanding of the love we should have, as described in the Love Chapter (1 Corinthians 13), expands our definition of love. As Christians, we are taught to define love by Christ's example. I suspect the only way we can love like this is to become more like Christ as we handle the problems we face in our marriages.

I don't think we enter marriage loving at this depth. I do believe, however, that as we cooperate with God in allowing the problems we encounter in marriage to shape and mold us into the image of Christ, the depth of our love will grow and deepen as our love takes on the character of Christ.

If we love our spouses according to chapter 13 of 1 Corinthians, and understand that the problems with which we wrestle in our marriages can be tools to make us more like Christ, then we can't be fooled by fiery darts—fiery darts that will cause us to feel we no longer love our spouse because there is no romantic motivation. Or fiery darts that tempt us to bail out of the marriage because our spouse no longer meets our needs or makes us happy. For example, if a woman has succumbed to the fiery dart that her marriage/husband is to be the source of her happiness, then she will form serious, unrealistic expectations regarding the purpose of marriage. She will operate under the delusion that her marriage exists to serve her wants and needs. Her husband, not Christ, will be expected to meet her desires for fulfillment and happiness.

Couples who have a secure grasp on God's design for marriage understand that their need for happiness and fulfillment must solely be met by Him. When that thought is secure in our minds, then we aren't depending on our spouse to make us happy and to affirm our self-worth. We release our spouse from the bondage of unrealistic expectations. Sure, we may get upset with him/her from time to time, but our relationship remains intact.

Gary Thomas is very clear on this point (especially from the wives' point of view).

> If you're trying to find your primary refuge in your husband, if you've centered your hope on him, if your security depends on his approval, and if you will do almost anything to gain his acceptance - then you've just given to a man what rightfully belongs to God alone.[10]

Forsaking Our Mission

In light of what this book has covered, I hope you can see more clearly the tragedy of divorce within the church. You see, when a Christian marriage fails the ramifications go far beyond the pain it inflicts upon the family. It says, to an unbelieving world, that being a Christian makes no difference in keeping a marriage intact. An unbelieving world cannot see that the reason the marriage failed was because that couple failed to understand that their marriage was a picture of Christ and His church. And they failed to understand how that picture applied to their marriage.

Couples tempted by divorce don't see their marriage as the means whereby God could fashion them to become more like Christ. They aren't aware of the glorious opportunity marriage gives them to forgive and be forgiven. They fail to understand how this element of forgiveness in marriage testifies of God's redemptive plan. They don't see how fiery darts have so dulled their sensitivity toward the things of God, that they honestly think they have no alternative other than divorce. Because, you see, that marriage was all about them. They just couldn't see that it was an instrument of God to conform them into the image of His Son and draw an unbelieving world to Himself!

Moving Forward

Again, I must emphasize the necessity to persevere in prayer and Bible study! We must grasp the fact that there is no other substitute. As we fellowship and worship in these two disciplines, everything we experience in life will be filtered through what we learn there. What we teach our children, how we define true love, how we view ourselves, our marriages, how we deal with difficulties, etc., will all be influenced by what we learn from God's Word and prayer.

Though we may have fallen prey to Satan's fiery darts, years ago, in our adolescence and suffer today in relationships that just don't measure up to God's ideal, as revealed in Scripture, all is not lost! Where you are right now is the best place to reenroll in God's classroom, to learn afresh how to correctly define love, and to understand the divine mysteries of marriage.

Begin by confessing your pride in going your own way and allowing society to have more of an influence on your understanding of love and marriage than you allowed God to have. Let God know you are willing to cooperate with Him, as He purges your mind of warped thinking and misconceptions influenced by the fiery darts of your past. Once this cleansing has taken place, you will have a fresh perspective on life. You will have a clearer understanding of God's intention and plan for you during adolescence, as He instructs you concerning true love. You will understand the holiness of marriage and will welcome the opportunity you have in this relationship to have God revealed to you and be conformed to Christ's image. You will establish new goals for yourself and your marriage. You will desire to learn more of Christ and your desire to please Him will motivate your thoughts and actions, especially when it comes to defining love and how to deal with conflict with your spouse.

As we learn more about Christ, through Bible study and prayer, we will gain wisdom and understanding for accessing God's power to attack the fiery darts that have gotten us off course and confused our thinking concerning what God desired to teach us during adolescence. Our marriages will be set on a new course, one that will make us holy and as a result, genuinely happy. We will find fulfillment in the plan God has for us. Marriages that adhere to God's standard offer the hope of heaven to a world that walks in darkness.

Afterword

The 3 R's of Fighting Fiery Darts
Use the following three steps as a quick
retaliation against persistent fiery darts:

1. Recognize
Examine the suspicious thought. If pondering on this
thought rouses up negative and destructive emotions, then
you are dealing with a fiery dart. Remember the intention
of a fiery darts is to obstruct your communication with God,
driving you further from prayer and God's Word.

2. Reject
As soon as you determine that the suspicious thought
is a fiery dart, reject it immediately. Remember, by allowing it
to remain, the poison of the fiery dart begins seeping into your
mind influencing the formation of negative attitudes, which
yield negative actions.

3. Replace
Every single time this fiery dart thought attempts to
infiltrate your mind, quickly and persistently replace it with
a Truth thought. There's a precise piece of scripture that
describes the character of these Truth thoughts.

> *Finally, brothers and sisters, whatever is true,*
> *whatever is noble, whatever is right, whatever is*
> *pure, whatever is lovely, whatever is admirable–*
> *if anything is excellent or praiseworthy–think*
> *about such things.* (Philippines 4:8 NIV)

For example:

Every time a fiery dart thought of fear attempts to invade your mind, quote the following Truth thought:

For God hath not given us the spirit of fear; but of power, and of love, and of a sound mind. (2 Timothy 1:7, KJV)

From this Truth thought you will proceed to form thoughts, attitudes, and actions based on power, love, and a sound mind.

1 Corinthians 13:1-7
(Referred to on page 74)

If I speak in the tongues of men and of angels, but have not love, I am only a resounding gong or a clanging cymbal. If I have the gift of prophecy and can fathom all mysteries and all knowledge, and if I have a faith that can move mountains, but have not love, I am nothing. If I give all I possess to the poor and surrender my body to the flames, but have not love, I gain nothing.

Love is patient, love is kind. It does not envy, it does not boast, it is not proud. It is not rude, it is not self-seeking, it is not easily angered, it keeps no record of wrongs. Love does not delight in evil but rejoices with the truth. It always protects, always trusts, always hopes, always perseveres. (NIV)

Romans 8:1-11
(Referred to on page 44)

Therefore, no condemnation now exists for those in Christ Jesus, because the Spirit's law of life in Christ Jesus has set you free from the law of sin and of death. What the law could not do since it was limited by the flesh, God did. He condemned sin in the flesh by sending His own Son in flesh like ours under sin's domain and as a sin offering, in order that the law's requirement would be accomplished in us who do not walk according to the flesh but according to the Spirit. For those who live according to the flesh think about the things of the flesh, but those who live according to the Spirit, about the things of the Spirit. For the mind-set of the flesh is death, but the mind-set of the Spirit is life and peace. For the mind-set of the flesh is hostile to God because it does not submit itself to God's law, for it is unable to do so. Those who are in the flesh cannot please God. You, however, are not in the flesh, but in the Spirit, since the Spirit of God lives in you. But if anyone does not have the Spirit of Christ, he does not belong to Him. Now, if Christ is in you, the body is dead because of sin, but the Spirit is life because of righteousness. And if the Spirit of Him who raised Jesus from the dead lives in you, then He who raised Christ from the dead will also bring your mortal bodies to life through His Spirit who lives in you.

Endnotes

The man without the Spirit does not accept the things that come from the Spirit of God, for they are foolishness to him, and he cannot understand them, because they are spiritually discerned. (1 Corinthians 2:14 NIV)

Because I realize that much of what God has taught me about fiery darts and the writing of this book are Truths that are spiritually discerned, I realize that the Enemy will attempt to prevent you from understanding "the things that come from the Spirit of God." To counter that please pray and seek the help of God's Spirit to enlighten your understanding as you read.

Perhaps there are those among my readers who have yet to commit their lives to Christ. Please consider the following:

- <u>Romans 5:8</u>, "But God demonstrates His own love toward us, in that while we were yet sinners, Christ died for us."

- <u>Romans 6:23</u>, "For the wages of sin is death but the free gift of God is eternal life in Christ Jesus our Lord."

- <u>Romans 10:9</u>, "that if you confess with your mouth Jesus as Lord, and believe in your heart that God raised Him for the dead, you shall be saved."

Prayer of Salvation: *Dear God, I believe that Jesus Christ is your Son and that He died and was raised from the dead. I confess my sin and my need for forgiveness and ask Jesus to save me. Thank you for giving me forgiveness, eternal life, and hope. Amen!*

Notes

Chapter Two: The Strength of Knowing Your Enemy

1. Henry, M. (1997). Nehemiah 6:1-2. *Matthew Henry's Commentary on the Bible*. Peabody, MA: Hendrickson Publishers.
2. Henry, M. (1997). Nehemiah 6:3. *Matthew Henry's Commentary on the Bible*. Peabody, MA: Hendrickson Publishers.
3. Henry, M. (1997). Nehemiah 6:4. *Matthew Henry's Commentary on the Bible*. Peabody, MA: Hendrickson Publishers.
4. Henry, M. (1997). Nehemiah 6:5-9. *Matthew Henry's Commentary on the Bible*. Peabody, MA: Hendrickson Publishers.
5. Henry, M. (1997). Nehemiah 6:8-9. *Matthew Henry's Commentary on the Bible*. Peabody, MA: Hendrickson Publishers.
6. Henry, M. (1997). Nehemiah 6:10. *Matthew Henry's Commentary on the Bible*. Peabody, MA: Hendrickson Publishers.
7. Henry, M. (1997). Nehemiah 6:15. *Matthew Henry's Commentary on the Bible*. Peabody, MA: Hendrickson Publishers.

Chapter Three: The Power of Negative Thinking

1. Leahy, R. (2003). Cognitive Therapy Techniques: A Practitioner's Guide. New York: Guilford Publications.
2. Moore, B. (2000). Breaking Free: Making Liberty in Christ a Reality in Life. Nashville, Tennessee: LifeWay Press. 50.

Chapter Four: Examination of Fiery Darts

1. *Webster's Eleventh Edition Collegiate Dictionary.* (2004). Springfield, MA: Merriam-Webster Inc.
2. Henry, M. (1997). Ephesians 6:16. *Matthew Henry's Commentary on the Bible.* Peabody, MA: Hendrickson Publishers.
3. Moore, B. (2000). *Breaking Free: Making Liberty in Christ a Reality in Life.* Nashville, Tennessee: LifeWay Press. 50.

Chapter Five: Being Aware of the Battle

1. Kehoe, Sean. Real Christianity Series, (2014) Book 7. Intro to The World, the flesh, and the Devil. retrieved on January 6, 2016. http://www.realchristianity.com/world-flesh-devil/introduction.html

2. HomosexualityAmericans Move Dramatically Toward Acceptance of Homosexuality. Retrieved on February 6, 2016 from http://www.norc.org/NewsEventsPublications/PressReleases/Pages/american-acceptance-of-homosexuality-gss-report.aspx

3. Kehoe, Sean. Real Christianity Series, (2014) Book 7. Intro to The World, the flesh, and the Devil. Retrieved on January 6, 2016. http://www.realchristianity.com/world-flesh-devil/introduction.html#sthash.A301dGH5.dpuf

Chapter Six: Telling the Difference

1. MacDonald, W. (1997). Matthew 4:1. *Believer's Bible Commentary: Old and New Testaments [electronic ed.], Logos Library System.* Nashville, Tennessee: Thomas Nelson.

2. MacDonald, W. (1997). Matthew 4:2-4. *Believer's Bible Commentary: Old and New Testaments [electronic ed.],*

Logos Library System. Nashville, Tennessee: Thomas Nelson.

3. MacDonald, W. (1997). Matthew 4:5-6. *Believer's Bible Commentary: Old and New Testaments [electronic ed.], Logos Library System*. Nashville, Tennessee: Thomas Nelson.
4. MacDonald, W. (1997). Matthew 4:7. *Believer's Bible Commentary: Old and New Testaments [electronic ed.], Logos Library System*. Nashville, Tennessee: Thomas Nelson.
5. MacDonald, W. (1997). Matthew 4:7. *Believer's Bible Commentary: Old and New Testaments [electronic ed.], Logos Library System*. Nashville, Tennessee: Thomas Nelson.
6. MacDonald, W. (1997). Matthew 4:8-10. *Believer's Bible Commentary: Old and New Testaments [electronic ed.], Logos Library System*. Nashville, Tennessee: Thomas Nelson.

Chapter Seven: Your Hope and Future

1. Kempis, T.A. (1966). *The Imitation of Christ.* Oak Harbor, WA: Logos Research Systems, Inc.

Chapter Eight: The Stirring of Adolescence

1. Harris, J. *I Kissed Dating Goodbye.* Sisters, Oregon: Multnomah Publishers. 29.
2. Holloway, B. (2008). Marriage Retreat. Snowbird Wilderness Outfitters, Andrews, N.C.

Chapter Nine: The Fiery Darts of Marriage

1. Murray, A. (2004). *The Holiest of All*. New Kensington, PA: Whitaker House. 6.

2. Murray, A. (2004). *The Holiest of All*. New Kensington, PA: Whitaker House. 6-7.
3. Robinson, B.A. (2009). U.S. divorce rates for various faith groups, age groups, geographic areas. Ontario Consultants on Religious Tolerance. Retrieved on March 30, 2010 from http://religioustolerance.org/chr_dira.htm.
4. Tupy, P.R. & Bare, J. (2006). SYMC Definition of Marriage. Save Your Marriage Central. Retrieved on March 30, 2010 from http://www.saveyourmarriagecentral.com/getactive/mfd/marriagedef.html
5. Thomas, G. (2000). *Sacred Marriage*. Grand Rapids, Michigan: Zondervan.
6. Bradley, R. (2002). *Help for the Struggling Marriage: What the Bible says about ending marriage by divorce*. Retrieved on March 30, 2010 from http://www.familyministries.com/marriage_purpose.htm
7. Thomas, G. (2000). *Sacred Marriage*. Grand Rapids, Michigan: Zondervan. 131.
8. Holloway, B. (2008). Marriage Retreat. Snowbird Wilderness Outfitters, Andrews, N.C.
9. Thomas, G. (2000). *Sacred Marriage*. Grand Rapids, Michigan: Zondervan. 150.
10. Thomas, G. (2000). *Sacred Marriage*. Grand Rapids, Michigan: Zondervan. 297.

Need
additional
copies?

FIERY DARTS:
SATAN'S WEAPON OF CHOICE

THIRD EDITION

JANET WARREN LANE

Janet Warren Lane

To learn more and purchase *Fiery Darts*, visit:

www.CertaPublishing.com/FieryDarts

Become a Fan on FaceBook

Visit my Blog: https://fierydarts.wordpress.com

Follow me on Twitter@LaneJanet

Certa
PUBLISHING